50 Days of Grace

Open Your Heart, Free Your Mind,
Dance with Life.

KRISTIN ROCCO

ISBN-13: 978-0-692-87455-4

www.50daysofgrace.com

A portion of proceeds goes to charity.

To all those who are on the path.

ACKNOWLEDGMENTS

My deepest gratitude to all those who have always supported me. Your love is the greatest gift of all.

I want to especially acknowledge my family and friends. I thank you from the bottom of my heart for always holding me in the light and for seeing my greatness.

Samir, thank you for all of it. Con todo mi corazon.

Casa Tranquila, you all rock! Thank you for standing by this project and for cheering it on from start to finish.

Brenda Isaac, you are an angel. Thank you for your profound coaching, encouragement and commitment to my growth and success in all areas of my life.

Keara Palmay, you were the first person to have given me advice and wisdom on self-publishing. Thank you for your inspiration and friendship.

Valerie Bishop, Russell Bishop and the Impact Hub Master Mind group, I feel so lucky and grateful for the opportunity to learn from you and with you. Your mentorship and guidance is a huge contribution to the completion of this book.

Dr. Louis Granirer, thank you for being an exceptional guide on my path of holistic health and wellbeing. I feel so blessed to be where I am today and you are a big part of that.

I would like to pay tribute to the personal and spiritual growth experiences and teachers that have brought out the best in me, connected me to the deepest parts of my being and allowed me to recognize, unleash, and share my gifts with the word.

HOW TO USE THIS BOOK

50 Days of Grace offers fifty daily choices to cultivate positive awareness. Each choice has greatly impacted my life for the better, and so I wish to share them with you. Here are two ways you can read this book:

1. Read one passage per day consecutively from beginning to end. Keep the book by your bedside and spend five to ten minutes in the morning as a beautiful way to start your day. Bring the words to life with intentionality and openness to receive the gifts they have to offer. Look for ways to implement each choice throughout your day and watch what happens with a new awareness. Before closing your eyes at night, reflect on the day. Creating time to journal will enrich and deepen your experience.

2. Randomly open up a page each day and see what choice is calling you. You can do this first thing in the morning or carry the book with you during the day. Use the same guide as above for how to implement and receive the passages.

You may also come up with your own way to use 50 Days of Grace.

However you choose to journey through this book, revisit it for gentle friendly reminders to allow ease and harmony into your life. I hope for *50 Days of Grace* to touch many lives. May it inspire inner peace, joy and fulfillment. May it evoke new insights and perspective. May it uplift your spirit and speak to your soul. May your heart be happy and your mind be free. We are all deserving and worthy. Here's to making each moment count.

The ultimate fall is the fall from Grace.

– Dale Halaway

Heaven on earth is a choice you must make, not a place you must find.

– Wayne Dyer

1.

Today I get to choose.

This is a blank slate.
This is the same blank slate
that exists in every moment of my life.
Each day when I open my eyes,
I am given the miracle of a fresh new start.
Each moment is a new opportunity.
To choose how I want to feel.
To choose how I want to live my life.
To choose how I want to experience my life.
Each moment is free from the past and
has not yet seen the future.
The only moment I have is now.
I leave the past behind, and
I trust that all is revealed in divine time.
I enter the now with a blank slate, and
I create exactly what I wish to create.
Today I get to choose.

When you live with an open heart, unexpected, joyful things happen.

– Oprah Winfrey

2.

Today I choose to open my heart.

When my heart is open,
I give love unconditionally
without expecting anything in return.
When my heart is open,
I receive love from others.
When my heart is open,
I receive life's blessings.
When my heart is closed,
I am shut off to the magic and gifts that life has to offer.
When my heart is open,
I act and think from a centered place.
When my heart is closed,
I act and think from an egoic place.
When my heart is open,
life's doors open up to me.
I flow through my days like water,
with grace and ease.
When my heart is open,
I have an infinite reservoir of compassion
for others and for myself.
I choose to practice opening my heart everywhere I go
and with everyone I meet.
Today I choose to open my heart.

Do you want to meet the love of your life? Look in the mirror.

– Byron Katie

3.

Today I choose to love myself.
I choose to love all aspects of myself.
I choose my body just the way it is
and just the way it isn't.
I choose to celebrate all of my parts.
Together they complete me.
I honor the light within me,
and I honor the dark within me.
Both are necessary and cannot exist without the other.
By choosing self love,
there is no need to compare myself to others.
With self love,
there is no room for putting myself down.
I do not desire to be different,
I am happy as I am.
I am perfect.
I am whole.
I am complete.
I love myself fully.
Today I choose to love myself.

Wisdom is knowing we are all one. Love is what it feels like and compassion is what it acts like.

– Ethan Walker III

4.

Today I choose to love all beings.

I see that we all come from the same source.

I see that we all return to the same source.

I choose to breakdown the barrier of physical appearance.

I choose to look below the surface and see into the soul.

When I strip away the layers,

I realize we are not so different.

At the core of all beings is love,

a desire to be loved and to give love.

Everyone deserves to receive love.

Every soul desires to give love.

To give love is to receive love.

As I stay open, the barriers of separation slowly fade.

By loving all beings, I am part of a greater movement.

Today I choose to love all beings.

5.

Today I choose to be in rhythm with nature.

Flowers bloom and fruits ripen in their own time.
If picked too soon,
fruit that promises sweetness
will be mouth-puckering sour.
With each season and without effort,
nature shifts accordingly.
The flowers, trees and animals all grow in their own time.
Leaves fall and blossoms bloom as the seasons change.
As a human being,
I undergo the same processes and cycles.
I too am part of this phenomenon.
I bud open and ripen with time just as nature intended.
I am in the exact phase and stage that
I am supposed to be in.
I trust in the divine timing of my life.
There is no need to fight or resist change.
Change is everywhere.
Change is constant.
There is no need to wonder
if I am where I am supposed to be
or doing what I am supposed to be doing.
What if I did not try so hard,
like an apple on a tree?
What if I let go of all the extra effort,
like a budding rose in the garden?
What if I trusted that I am naturally growing and
blossoming exactly as nature intended?

Sometimes I so badly want to know the outcome.
Life is a great mystery,
revealing one moment at a time.
I trust and nestle into my process of growth and unfolding.
Nature is my teacher.
I become the sweet fruit
that naturally falls ripened from a tree,
rather than the tart fruit
that is picked prematurely.
I become the beautiful flower,
with petals that peel open in due time.
One cannot force a flower open
to reveal its true beauty inside.
I trust in the nature within me.
My life is unfolding perfectly.
I am exactly where I am supposed to be.
Right here, right now.
Today I choose to be in rhythm with nature.

I have found that if you love life, life will love you back.

– Arthur Rubinstein

6.

Today I choose to love life.

Life.
It is happening.
Right now.
Moment by moment.
Love it or hate it, life goes on.
And so do I.
Run with it or run from it, life goes on.
And so do I.
When I choose to love life,
life loves me.
When I choose to love others,
others love me.
Love solves problems.
Love provides answers.
Love will guide me when I am lost.
Love will protect me when I am harmed.
I deserve every ounce of happiness that life has to offer.
By loving life, I feel fully alive.
I am joyous.
I am free.
I can hear my heart sing.
Today I choose to love life.

Even after all this time the sun never says to the earth,
"You owe me." Look what happens with a love like that. It
lights the whole sky.

– Hafiz

7.

Today I choose to love my body.

My body is a temporary vessel,
allowing me to experience life on earth.
What is me?
Me is not my body.
Me is eternal.
My body is temporary.
Aging is natural.
We are nature.
If I resist aging, I will suffer.
I honor my body, my sacred temple.
It deserves to be treated with love and care.
It deserves to be spoken to kindly.
Today I stand before a mirror,
face to face with my own reflection.
I look into my eyes and say out loud, "I am beautiful."
I have compassion for myself if this feels challenging.
Each day, over and over I affirm, "I am beautiful."
I wrap loving arms around my body.
I scan my body from head to toe,
directing love and gratitude to each part.
I am thankful for my body exactly the way it is.
I choose to give up any desire to be different.
Those desires only cause harm.
All bodies are precious.
Today I choose to love my body.

When receiving intuitive information through your body,
the more you listen, the more you hear.

– Karen Whitaker

8.

Today I choose to listen to my body.

By tuning into my body,
I can learn what part of myself needs
care, attention or fine-tuning.
The emotional and physical bodies
have a direct relationship to one another.
They are always communicating with me.
At first they speak in subtle whispers.
When I do not listen they knock louder,
often manifesting as ill health.
Carl Jung said, "the gods visit us through illness."
I am committed to loving, listening to and
cherishing my body.
As I develop a more intimate relationship with my body,
I connect deeper with all of its parts and their needs.
With practice, listening becomes preventative medicine.
Today I choose to listen to my body.

Health is a state of complete harmony of the body, mind and spirit.

– B.K.S. Iyengar

9.

Today I choose to commit to one new healthy habit.

Rather than postponing until tomorrow
or when the time is right,
I start now.
The time is always right
to take care of my health and wellbeing.
A new year, a new way of life and a new me can
begin any day.
I choose to take a stand for myself.
I stand for my personal empowerment.
If I put off healthy change today,
I will most likely put it off tomorrow too.
There is no better moment than the present.
Today I choose to commit to one new healthy habit.

There is no love without forgiveness, and there is no forgiveness without love.

– Bryant H. McGill

10.

Today I choose to forgive myself.

I choose to be free.
I am the only one keeping myself
locked up, constrained, alone.
I am the only one who can set myself free.
Nobody else has the key.
Each day is a new day,
a new opportunity to be who I want to be.
I honor my past.
I cherish and take with me the lessons I learned.
I use them to guide me in the future.
I find peace in knowing that
everything happens for a reason.
I am here to learn and grow.
Everyone has done things that they are not proud of,
that have caused them or others harm.
It is what I choose to do with my past that
creates my destiny.
I can stay stuck in regret or I can forgive and move on.
Forgiveness opens the door to new life.
It is time to push the door open, spread my wings and
set myself free.
Today I choose to forgive myself.

It's one of the greatest gifts you can give yourself, to forgive. Forgive everybody.

– Maya Angelou

11.

Today I choose to forgive someone.

I see that we all have underlying reasons
for the way we act and behave.
I recognize that when someone acts in a way
that is unaligned with love,
he or she is projecting his or her own suffering.
Everyone has some level of pain deep down within.
When I hold grudges or resentment against others,
I am the one who suffers the most.
It generates negativity in my body, mind and spirit.
Knowing this, I open myself to forgiving others.
I trust that compassion and love will guide me.
No matter what was said or done,
I choose to open my heart
and be a gateway for healing.
I choose to look below the surface of anger or negativity.
Today I think of someone who has upset or harmed me.
I will open my heart to them.
I can do this in my thoughts,
a letter, over the phone, or in person.
A simple shift within me,
has the power to change external circumstances.
The smallest actions can make a big difference.
Today I choose to forgive someone.

12.

Today I choose to be vulnerable.

Being vulnerable means sharing myself,
truthfully and honestly.
It requires opening and speaking from the heart.
It means revealing aspects of myself
that I am scared to show.
Being vulnerable can be difficult.
Especially if I am used to hiding my true feelings.
I take the mask off that has been covering up what is inside,
My true self.
The truth is, all human beings struggle from time to time.
Everyone experiences unpleasant emotions.
This is what makes us human.
I trust that good things come from
letting my guard down and allowing others in.
When I am vulnerable,
I invite others to let their guard down as well.
When I am vulnerable,
I open myself up to receiving support and love.
When I am vulnerable,
I create deeper bonds with others.
By sharing with one another,
I see that I am never truly alone.
I see that my struggles are not so unique,
they are a part of life.

Being vulnerable takes practice.
With time, I become more comfortable sharing myself.
Being vulnerable sets me free.
Being vulnerable connects me with others.
Being vulnerable is healing.
Today I choose to be vulnerable.

We live in a wonderful world that is full of beauty, charm and adventure. There is no end to the adventures that we can have if only we seek them with our eyes open.

– Jawaharlal Nehru

13.

Today I choose to see life as an adventure.
What would it be like to wake up everyday,
excited for the great mystery that is ahead?
Everyday there is
something new to discover,
someone new to meet,
something new to learn.
When I choose an adventurous mindset,
I shift the perspective that life is repetitive and mundane.
I open myself up to new experiences and new friends.
I open myself up to learning and growth opportunities.
I feel excited about the possibilities that exist.
They are infinite.
Today I choose to see life as an adventure.

If you can dream it, do it.

– Walt Disney

14.

Today I choose to believe I can.

My mind is either my greatest ally or my biggest enemy.
I choose to make it my ally,
to be on the same team.
My mind holds great power to create.
All dreams start with a single thought and spark of belief.
With the power of my mind,
I can do anything I believe in.
Belief is a superpower that all humans have.
I believe that I can, and so I will.
I do whatever it takes to build my belief.
Every time I doubt myself,
I choose to switch my thoughts and dialogue to
believing in myself.
My thoughts are like radio stations.
I choose to turn the dial and
tune into words of encouragement.
It's ok if I don't believe in myself at first.
I simply continue choosing supportive thoughts.
With practice, my belief grows.
By building my belief,
I will soon believe.
Today I choose to believe I can.

Perfect happiness is a beautiful sunset, the giggle of a grandchild, the first snowfall. It's the little things that make happy moments, not the grand events. Joy comes in sips, not gulps.

– Sharon Draper

15.

Today I choose to appreciate the little things.

Sometimes it is the little things that mean the most.
They hold much more significance than
I give them credit for.
I practice not taking the little things for granted.
What little things can I be grateful for today?
A smile from a stranger.
A cool breeze.
Clean water to drink.
A bed to sleep in.
A slobbering kiss from my dog,
who loves me unconditionally.
Everyday is full of little things
and little moments to appreciate.
Today I choose to appreciate the little things

The most important relationship in your life is the relationship you have with yourself. Because no matter what happens, you will always be with yourself.

– Diane Von Furstenberg

16.

Today I choose to be my own best friend.

Rather than depending on others to have fun with,
to feel loved or to be happy,
I depend on myself.
Today I am my own best friend.
Today I am my own adventure buddy.
Today I discover joy in spending time with myself.
Today I speak kindly to myself.
Today I think loving thoughts about myself.
It is one of life's greatest lessons,
to generate total fulfillment within myself.
It is a real treat to spend time with myself.
To be content with myself
To feel total love for myself.
Today I choose to be my own best friend.

Doing the best at this moment puts you in the best place
for the next moment.

– Oprah Winfrey

17.

Today I choose to do the best that I can.

I choose to be accepting and proud of my efforts.
Some days I show up 100%,
Some days less.
I alleviate stress and tension by
dropping the need for perfection.
I acknowledge that I cannot always be on my A game.
That is ok.
I find ease accepting that doing my best each day is enough.
I feel unstoppable on the days that I am in rock star mode.
I am compassionate on the days when I need a break.
It is ok to cut myself some slack.
Today I choose to do the best that I can.

18.

Today I choose to be confident in my decisions.

Do it or don't do it.
Say it or don't say it.
Bigger decisions may require
more thought and consideration
than the smaller day to day decisions.
Regardless of the decision,
lingering for too long in indecision
leaves me feeling stuck.
It takes over my mind and drains my energy.
Indecision is like a glass of water.
When knocked over,
It spills everywhere.
It spreads into other areas of my life.
Assessing the possible outcomes of my actions is wise.
Teeter tottering back and forth between what to do
is counterproductive.
Making and trusting my decisions is a practice.
The more decisions I make and action I take,
the more I learn about myself.
My intuition strengthens.
My self-confidence grows.
It is ok if I make a decision that
leads to an undesired outcome.

By knowing what I do not want,
I know more about what I do want.
I am closer to where I want to be.
I find success in taking consistent action.
Today I choose to be confident in my decisions.

Pause for a moment and realize how much progress you have made. Be proud of yourself; celebrate yourself.

– Roxana Jones

19.

Today I choose to acknowledge myself.

I am the star of my life.
Some days I struggle to get out of bed.
Some days I stay in bed.
Either way, I still show up.
I have weathered many storms,
climbed many mountains,
explored uncharted territory.
When was the last time I acknowledged myself?
Do I put myself down?
Is it easier for me to acknowledge and praise others?
There are many amazing things about me.
I choose to love and honor myself.
I am proud of who I am.
What can I be grateful for?
What can I give myself a pat on the back for?
I am deserving and worthy of acknowledgement.
It doesn't matter what I have done or
who I have been in the past.
The good news about the past is it's in the past.
What matters is what I am doing and
who I am being in the present moment.
I do not need to wait for someone else to acknowledge me.
Today I choose to acknowledge myself.

20.

Today I choose to honor my word.

How am I with keeping commitments to myself?
To others?
Do I make excuses, cancel plans or simply ignore
what I said I was going to do?
Whether it is working out, eating healthy,
making plans, an assignment, or cleaning my space,
keeping my word builds inner power.
Keeping my word creates healthy habits.
Life flows when I am in integrity with my word.
When I do not keep my word time after time,
I am living out of integrity.
Life's flow dams up when I am out of integrity.
When I do not keep my word,
there are consequences.
People lose trust and confidence in me.
This creates a way of being and a reality that
is not in my favor.
What kind of message am I putting out into the Universe?
Do my actions affirm
I am accountable and deserving of trust?
Sometimes I genuinely cannot keep a commitment
because of unforeseen circumstances or
I need to take care of myself.

The best way to handle these situations is
with honesty, not excuses.
When I am honest,
I honor and respect others and myself.
By evaluating my reasons,
I can determine if they are excuses or
genuine reasons.
Today I choose to honor my word.

Everyone is a star and deserves a chance to shine.

– Marilyn Monroe

21.

Today I choose to let others shine.

I drop the need to be seen and heard.
I allow someone else the space to be seen and heard.
I drop the idea of self-importance and status.
I allow someone else to shine and be recognized.
What a gift it is to witness someone else
receive recognition and praise.
I enjoy seeing others light up.
I enjoy seeing others feel worthy and acknowledged.
I practice feeling happy for others,
rather than jealous and competitive.
Standing for someone else's empowerment
is to be fully empowered.
Today I choose to let others shine.

Feelings or emotions are the universal language and are to be honored. They are the authentic expression of who you are at your deepest place.

– Judith Wright

22.

Today I choose to accept my emotions.

I choose to welcome all feelings,
even the unpleasant ones.
I embrace them, and I befriend them.
When I turn away from pain and discomfort,
I create constriction in my mind and body.
When I turn towards pain and discomfort,
I turn towards healing.
I open up the door and let all feelings in,
like a neighbor coming over to say "hello."
I leave my judgments behind, and
I spend time with my feelings.
I stay curious and open.
By acknowledging, accepting and embracing my emotions,
they will run their course.
By doing the opposite,
they stick around until I am ready to be with them.
What I resist persists.
Running away or suppressing does no good.
When I stuff my emotions down,
they become like a volcano waiting to erupt.
My emotions are what make me human.
The ability to feel is a beautiful thing.
Today I choose to accept my emotions.

Sometimes surrender means giving up trying to understand
and becoming comfortable with not knowing.

– Eckhart Tolle

23.

Today I choose to surrender.

When life becomes a struggle,
when all of nature's forces
seem like they are against me,
when all of my efforts are not working,
this is the time to surrender.
When I surrender, I step aside.
I allow a greater force to come through and take over.
Surrendering requires courage.
Surrendering requires faith.
Surrendering requires giving up control.
Surrendering requires detaching from
how I think things should be.
Surrendering does not mean giving up or defeat.
Surrendering is a dance between doing and not doing,
between action and patience.
I become an observer of my life and how it is unfolding.
I trust in the journey.
Surrendering is when I truly begin living.
Today I choose to surrender.

We don't stop playing because we grow old; we grow old because we stop playing.

– George Bernard Shaw

24.

Today I choose playfulness.
Every day is an opportunity to welcome in playfulness.
What was life like before it became so serious?
There was a time when life felt more like a friend and
less of a threat.
Just because I have more responsibilities,
does not mean the fun has to be over.
Now is the perfect time to rediscover the
days of feeling playful and having fun.
When I choose a playful perspective and way of being,
life is more enjoyable.
When I play with life,
life plays with me.
What responsibility or activity can I approach like a game?
Today I choose playfulness.

Better to lose count while naming your blessings than to
lose your blessings to counting your troubles.

– Maltbie Davenport Babcock

25.

Today I choose to see what is right.

What I focus on creates my reality.
When I focus on what is wrong I struggle,
life seems hard.
When I focus on what is right life feels great.
I am choosing a positive mindset.
What is right and what is wrong are always available to me.
Some days are indeed more challenging than others.
If I am intentional with my thoughts,
I can always look for what is right.
Being alive is what is right.
Knowing people I care about is what is right.
Knowing people who care about me is what is right.
Getting from point a to point b safely is what is right.
Having food to eat and water to drink is what is right.
The more I work the muscle of focusing on what is right,
the easier it becomes.
The ego loves to find things that are wrong.
The soul loves to find things that are right.
I choose to align with my soul,
I focus on all that is going right in life.
What is right is always present,
even when it doesn't seem so.
I just have to choose it.
Today I choose to see what's right.

Every thought we think is creating our future.

– Louise Hay

26.

Today I choose to be responsible for my thoughts.

The mind consists of many voices.
I have the choice to believe what they are saying or
to simply observe what they are saying.
I can choose to witness the different voices and thoughts,
Instead of reacting to them or believing them all to be true.
No matter what is happening in my mind,
I can always think a new thought.
Positive thinking leads to positive outcomes.
Negative attracts more negative.
Positivity is my greatest resource.
I choose to be intentional with my thoughts.
I choose my thoughts wisely.
I am responsible.
I can either be a prisoner of the mind or
a conscious empowered human being.
Today I choose to be responsible for my thoughts.

Exploration is really the essence of the human spirit.

– Frank Borman

27.

Today I choose to explore somewhere new.

There are always new places to discover near and far,
both internally and externally.
A park, a city, my mind, or my heart.
I choose to explore the world.
I choose to explore myself.
Exploration evokes excitement, expansion and growth.
When I am not growing I become stagnant and lethargic.
My zest for life is not so zesty.
My inner and outer worlds provide
endless opportunities to explore.
I pick a destination and begin the exploration.
Today I choose to explore somewhere new.

The best way to find yourself is to lose yourself in the
service of others.

– Mahatma Gandhi

28.

Today I choose to devote myself to service.

I choose to serve others before myself.
Contribution feeds the soul.
I choose to lend a helping hand.
To someone I know or a stranger.
To a four year old or ninety-four year old.
To the wealthiest person on the block or
the person who's home is a park bench.
Acts of service are the fastest way
to get out of my head,
to step out of my drama,
to shift my energy, mood and state of mind.
Today I commit to finding someone to help,
someone to do something nice for.
Today I choose to devote myself to service.

You are in a much better position to serve others when
your basic needs are met and your tank is full.

– Michael Hyatt

29.

Today I choose to be selfish.

I give myself permission to have a day dedicated to me.
Today I tend to my own needs rather than everyone else's.
It is necessary for my wellbeing.
I take time for personal care.
To do something nice for myself.
When my own well is full,
when I feel nurtured and taken care of,
I am able to show up for others in a much larger way.
If I am used to putting others needs before my own,
This may feel challenging.
I take a moment to be quiet and still.
I go inward and ask,
what do I need right now?
What is my body asking for?
What would make me happy?
Today I honor myself.
Today I choose to be selfish.

30.

Today I choose to take a trip down memory lane.

This is a healing process.
From the moment I entered the world until now,
my life's memories are stored within.
Those memories and experiences shape who I am today.
Some memories I have chosen to block out or forget,
to avoid feeling pain.
Other memories I welcome freely,
as they bring a smile to my face.
I practice acknowledging the hard times.
By spending time with these memories,
I recognize and heal the hurt I still carry.
There are many ways to evoke this process.
I can look at old photos.
I can share with someone I feel safe with and trust.
I can create a peaceful, soothing, quiet space
to call forth and be with my past.
I can hire a professional coach, light worker or therapist.
I can research therapeutic healing services.
The options are plentiful.
If I feel stuck and unsure,
prayer and intention is a great place to start.

I ask for guidance on my healing path.
Please lead me to that which will heal
any pain or wounds within my heart.
It is easier to call upon the happy times.
It is courageous to call upon the darker times.
It is important to honor all of life's experiences.
To find peace in each moment.
To get closure where closure is needed.
To move forward with freedom and ease.
I trust that everything has lead me to where I am today.
Everything that happens is for
my own growth and highest good.
I am grateful for it all.
Today I choose to take a trip down memory lane.

Holding on is believing that there's a past; letting go is knowing that there's a future.

– Daphne Rose Kingma

31.

Today I choose to let something go.

If I am ready to grow,
I have to be willing and prepared to let something go.
This can be limiting beliefs, negative self talk,
unhealthy habit patterns, relationships, a job,
and anything else that does not support my evolution.
Sometimes letting go feels uncomfortable.
It can bring up a lot of emotions
I trust that when I shed the things that do not serve me,
I am contributing to my process in a good way.
I learn to be comfortable with the uncomfortable,
knowing that all things pass.
I trust that by letting something go,
I create space for something new.
I will be guided to the people, places and things
that are aligned with my growth and
my soul's deepest desires.
I will be lead to new possibilities of happiness and ease.
Life is always presenting opportunities to grow and let go.
Will I choose it or resist it or
will I choose to embrace it?
Today I choose to let something go.

32.

Today I choose to enter the silence.
In the silence there is a vast world.
There are lessons, insights and self-discovery.
My outer world is becoming more advance each day.
Sometimes it is easy to get swept away with
the hustle and bustle.
I am grateful for new technology, the media and
my social environments.
On the other hand,
It can be over stimulating, overwhelming and bombarding.
I have learned to adapt and speed up with the times.
I must also relearn to slow down.
I create time to be quiet,
to check in with myself.
I listen, I nourish, I replenish, I rest, and I rejuvenate.
I can always choose and commit to entering the silence.
For three minutes, an hour or an entire day.
Whatever time I have is enough.
When I take time to simply be silent,
I honor my body, mind and spirit.
The days I can barely find time to eat lunch,
are the days it is most important to take a pause.
There is always at least sixty seconds in a day that
I can dedicate to my well-being.

I Pause.
I close my eyes.
I focus on my breath.
I am still.
Breathe in. Breathe out.
Today I choose to enter the silence.

When you change the way you look at things, the things
you look at change.

– Wayne Dyer

33.

Today I choose to accept everything exactly the way it is.
Do I complain about life circumstances?
Do I complain about others?
Do I wish that things or people are different than they are?
What do I complain about the most?
How much suffering does this create for me?
What would life be like without the complaints?
There are always two perspectives,
two ways to see the same picture.
Is my glass half full or half empty?
If my glass is half empty,
my context will be from a place of lack and negativity.
Do I want my point of attraction to be rooted in
non-acceptance, complaints and lack?
Or do I want my point of attraction to come from
acceptance, positivity and abundance?
What I focus on I attract.
My thoughts create my reality.
I choose to see the positive perspective in all situations.
Life is much more pleasant when my glass is half full.
This is living life powerfully.
Today I choose to accept everything exactly the way it is.

Slow down and everything you are chasing will come
around and catch you.

– John De Paola

34.

Today I choose to take the pressure off.

When it comes to deadlines,
do I put excess unhealthy pressure on myself?
Some pressure is helpful.
It can stimulate motivation and drive.
A lot of pressure can be harmful,
effecting my health and wellbeing.
When I relax and trust that I am doing my very best,
I allow the pressure to subside.
Without excessive pressure boiling inside of me,
I can still be productive.
My work becomes less of a burden.
I am able to stay calm and carry on.
I choose to find healthy ways to
deal with stress and pressure like
mediation, yoga, exercise, deep breaths, rest, a walk outside.
Today I choose to take the pressure off.

In the midst of movement and chaos, keep stillness
inside of you.

– Deepak Chopra

35.

Today I choose to stay centered.

When I am centered,
I do not try to control external circumstances.
When I am centered, I am unshakable and unbreakable.
When I am centered, I can weather any storm.
When I am centered, I feel safe and protected.
When I am centered, I act and speak from my heart.
When I am centered, I can handle negativity and aversion.
When I am centered, I accept things not going my way.
When I am centered, I choose positive thoughts.
When I am centered,
I give empowering meaning to challenging events.
When I am centered, I know that I cannot fail.
When I am centered,
I trust that everything is an opportunity to learn and grow.
During times of chaos or distress,
finding my center is top priority.
I stop everything.
I close my eyes.
I focus on my breath.
I connect to my heart.
I connect to my inner source.
Today I choose to stay centered.

Action is the bridge between your current reality and your wildest dreams.

– Keara Palmay

36.

Today I choose to be complete.

Being complete with someone or something
removes barriers.
It is the settling of unfinished business.
What thoughts or words have been left unsaid?
What Intentions and goals have I been ignoring?
What unresolved disagreements with others
are still lingering?
What dreams have I given up on
that still whisper my name?
I say what my heart wants to say.
I do what my heart wants to do.
When I ignore or avoid what is incomplete,
I create blocks in my life.
Little by little,
I begin to clean up and tackle
incompletions and unfinished business.
It is never too late.
The time is always now.
Now is all I have.
Today I choose to be complete.

37.

Today I choose to break through resistance.

What have I been putting off?

What am I avoiding?

A long overdue task?

A new adventure?

Reaching a goal?

Confronting a problem?

Resolving a conflict?

A difficult conversation?

By taking action, I liberate myself.

What are the reasons why I do not want to do something?

I acknowledge my reasons.

I have compassion for my reasons.

I see how my reasons hold me back.

It is time to move forward,

to let go of my reasons.

I reclaim my power by taking action.

Action nourishes my

happiness, freedom, success, and peace.

Action propels me forward.

I make a list of everything that I have been resisting.

Next to each line,

I write down one action I can take that moves me forward.

If action scares me, I start with smaller steps.
Each time I take even the smallest action,
I build momentum and create energy to take more action.
I see that with each action taken,
I am closer to where I want to be.
The more action I take,
the less resistance I have to being in action.
When I am in action, the Universe responds.
I find ways to celebrate every time I am in action.
This is positive reinforcement.
Today I choose to breakthrough resistance.

Chaos always comes before creation.

– Michael Meade

38.

Today I choose to see breakdowns as the gateway to breakthroughs

Breakdowns are necessary.
Breakdowns are opportunities to grow and initiate change.
Breakdowns allow me to say,
"Enough is enough! No more!"
This is the moment that transformation happens.
New choices are made,
new beliefs are created,
new actions are taken.
I do not resist or run away from breakdowns.
I choose to turn towards my breakdowns.
To accept them.
To learn from them.
I have faith that on the other side is a breakthrough.
Today I choose to see breakdowns
as the gateway to breakthroughs.

39.

Today I choose a new way of being.

What way of being is not serving me?

What kind of life would I create if no barriers existed?

What is worth living for?

What way of being would give me a deeper reason to
wake up each day?

What way of being would put a pep in my step?

I acknowledge the ways of being that no longer serve me,
I let them go.

I step into my power as a human being.

I choose a way of being that
inspires, motivates and excites me.

Who I choose to be is something
I have complete control over.

It is a choice I get to make each moment.

Who I choose to be shapes my actions,
ultimately shaping my destiny.

If I do not consciously and intentionally choose
who I am being every day,

I allow lower vibrational ways of being
to erupt during times of stress or upset.

I allow life's circumstances to have control over me.

By choosing to be loving and kind,

I don't loose my cool in traffic or when someone is rude.

I cannot be angry if I am choosing to be loving and kind.

I get to create an extraordinary life
with who I choose to be.
Being someone is the purpose of my existence,
hence the name human being.
I choose to step into something worth living for.
For myself, my loved ones and the entire world.
Today I choose a new way of being.

Beauty begins the moment you decide to be yourself.

– Coco Chanel

40.

Today I choose to be secure with myself.

Do I seek approval from others
to make up for the lack of security I have within myself?
Do I question my decisions?
Do I question myself?
What are they thinking of me?
Am I good enough?
Do I look ok?
Do they like me?
What would life be like if
I had more faith and trust in myself?
I would live more freely.
I would love more tenderly.
I would speak more openly.
I would let go of worry and doubt.
I would take more risks.
I would hold back just a little less.
I would walk towards my dreams.
I would know that
I am worthy, deserving and capable.
Rather than seeking approval from others,
it is time to approve myself.
I am already perfect just the way I am.
Today I choose to be secure with myself.

There is a voice that doesn't use words. Listen.

– Rumi

41.

Today I choose to trust my intuition.

When I came to this earth,
I was granted the gift of intuition.
It is a special power that guides me on my path.
It is an internal built in guidance system.
It helps me navigate the unknown.
My intuition nudges me in the direction of
my highest calling.
It leads me to people and experiences that
contribute to my growth and expansion.
When I don't listen to my intuition,
sometimes the outcome may cause struggle or pain.
This is part of the learning process,
learning to trust myself.
I practice listening to the whispers of my inner voice.
Sometimes my intuition speaks through strong feelings,
like a gut instinct.
With practice and intent,
I learn to recognize when a feeling is directing me
towards or away from something.
When making decisions, I tune into my heart and my body.
I find stillness and quiet within, and I listen for direction.
My intuition is always communicating with me.
By honoring my intuition, I honor my heart and soul.
I honor my path.
Today I choose to trust my intuition.

There are no seven wonders of the world in the eyes of a
child. There are seven million.

– Walt Streightiff

42.

Today I choose to see life through the eyes of a child.
Children are in awe of everything that surrounds them.
Babies stare at their own hands and feet for hours,
in such wonder.
They embody a presence to everything in sight.
To do the same, this requires slowing down.
It requires taking my time with what is in front of me.
Humans today are moving through life at a faster pace.
Rushing from moment to moment.
Wanting to be there instead of here.
Have I been too busy to stop and smell the flowers?
Do I notice the beauty that is all around me?
Am I missing the small opportunities to be grateful?
When speaking with others is my mind wandering,
or am I fully engaged and truly listening?
The present moment is full of magic.
The present moment is an ocean of possibility.
I choose to look at life in awe and wonder.
After all, it is quite magnificent.
Today I choose to see life through the eyes of a child.

What a liberation to realize that the "voice in my head" is not who I am. Who am I then? The one who sees that.

– Eckhart Tolle

43.

Today I choose to see that I am not my mind.

I choose to drop the
"I should haves" and "I shouldn't haves."
I choose to drop the "I am not enoughs."
They don't belong to me, they belong to the mind.
The mind is reactive.
The mind tries to trick and confuse me.
I bring awareness to my mind and its thoughts.
I choose to disregard the disempowering voices.
I cannot get rid of the mind,
I learn to coexist with it.
When the mind chimes in with negativity
I simply say, "that is mind."
The more I acknowledge mind as mind and not as me,
the less power it has.
This is a moment-to-moment practice.
The more I practice,
the more I listen from and am guided by my heart.
Mind lives in worry, fear and doubt.
Heart lives in peace, love and trust.
My heart tells the truth.
My heart always guides me in the right direction.
I am a soul, I am not a mind.
I reclaim my soul power.
Mind no longer runs the show.
Today I choose to see that I am not my mind.

44.

Today I choose equanimity.
Am I attached to feeling good,
to the pleasant experiences?
Do I resist not feeling good,
pushing away the unpleasant experiences?
Craving the highs and fighting the lows
creates suffering within me.
Do I bounce back and forth between
two-sides of a spectrum;
good or bad,
happy or sad,
joyful or angry?
By choosing equanimity,
I practice living in the middle.
Balanced.
Accepting all that comes my way.
Enjoying the highs and allowing them to pass.
Accepting the lows and allowing them to pass.
Unattached.
The highs will come again.
The lows will come again.
Instead of judging feeling good as good and
feeling bad as bad,
I practice removing the labels.

I observe all feelings that come each day.
I appreciate all of life's cycles.
I welcome the ups and the downs.
Both are inevitable.
Both are necessary.
Both are always passing.
I appreciate sunshine because I know rain.
I appreciate rain because I know sunshine.
I experience the natural ebb and flow that
my very self is made up of.
Today I choose equanimity

It is only the farmer who faithfully plants seeds in the
Spring, who reaps a harvest in the Autumn.

– B. C. Forbes

45.

Today I choose to plant a new seed.

Every goal or dream begins with
a single spark of inspiration.
It begins first in my thoughts.
What do I want to create?
What change do I wish to see in myself or in my life?
A seed planted in my mind
grows over time when fed with
belief, determination and action.
By watering my seeds every day,
I watch them grow and blossom.
I practice patience along the way.
Today I choose to plant a new seed

46.

Today I choose abundance.

Thoughts create reality.

What I think is what I am.

Focusing on abundance generates abundance.

Abundance comes in many forms,

not just as money or possessions.

Nature, health and love are forms of abundance.

If I want to attract more abundance in my life,

I must first feel abundant on the inside.

If I want to attract more abundance in my life,

I must feel worthy of receiving it.

I visualize what abundance looks like.

I feel an unlimited supply of resources within me.

I feel an unlimited supply of love within me.

I feel an unlimited supply of joy within me.

I feel an unlimited supply of prosperity within me.

I have an overflowing well of abundance within me.

I open myself up to receive all forms of wealth.

I am deserving of all forms of wealth.

I am worthy of all forms of wealth.

If I want to attract more abundance in my life,

I must acknowledge and be grateful for

the abundance that already exists.

I see the abundance that surrounds me.

If I want to attract more abundance in my life,
I must replace jealousy and judgment with
true happiness for other's success and prosperity.
By practicing these principles,
the feeling of abundance grows inside of me.
When I feel abundant, I give to others more freely.
When I feel abundant, I give to others from the heart.
When I give love, I receive love.
When I give support, I receive support.
When I give kindness, I receive kindness.
Today I choose abundance.

Life is a journey, not a destination.

– Ralph Waldo Emerson

47.

Today I choose to see that life is a journey.

There is no final destination.
There are many journeys that
make up one big journey.
There are many destinations that
make up the tapestry of my life.
Every beginning has an end.
Every end has a beginning.
To reach a final destination would mean that life is over.
I learn to enjoy the process,
all of the twists and turns.
I learn to be comfortable exactly where I am right now.
I practice slowing down
rather than rushing to some finish line.
I practice noticing and appreciating the little things.
I practice gratitude for all that I have each day.
I am exactly where I am supposed to be.
Life can be an epic journey if I allow it to be.
Today I choose to see that life is a journey.

Home isn't a place, it's a feeling.

– Cecelia Ahern

48.

Today I choose to see that home is inside of me.

No matter where I am physically,
I find comfort in knowing that home is a feeling I cultivate.
No matter where I am.
No matter who I am with.
No matter what I am doing.
I relax in knowing that home is wherever I am.
Roman philosopher Pliny the Elder said,
"Home is where the heart is."
This is a wise truth to practice and live by.
I cultivate the feeling of home within.
I carry it wherever I go.
If I feel homesick or lost,
I simply close my eyes and find home inside.
In my heart.
I focus on my breath.
I affirm that I am home.
Today I choose to see that home is inside of me.

The open heart sees, feels and absorbs the beauty of the world.

– Sonia Choquette

49.

Today I choose love as my guiding light.
When I choose love, there is no room for hate.
When I choose love, there is compassion for myself.
When I choose love, there is compassion for others.
When I choose love, I overcome fear.
When I choose love, I heal.
When I choose love, I dissolve barriers with others.
When I choose love, I am open to receiving.
When I choose love, I can allow others in.
When I choose love, I find solutions.
When I choose love, I am one with all.
When I choose love, miracles happen.
When I choose love, I create a better world.
When I choose love, I am a force to be reckoned with.
When I choose love, there is no fighting.
When I choose love, I feel peace.
When in doubt, I choose love.
Love will always show me the way.
Today I choose love as my guiding light.

Drop the idea of becoming someone, because you are already a masterpiece. You cannot be improved. You have only to come to it, to know it, to realize it.

– Osho

50.

Today I choose to see that I am a miracle.

I am enough just the way I am.

The odds of being born exactly when and where I was
are extraordinary.

To be precise, they are about
*1 in 400,000,000,000.

Isn't that miraculous?

I am part of an interconnected web of breathing life.

Each living participant is a unique offering to the whole.

I don't have to try to be something.

I already am.

I don't have to try to be special.

I already am.

I don't have to prove anything.

Being alive is proof.

I choose to celebrate my life.

I choose to celebrate me.

I am a gift to the world.

Today I choose to see that I am a miracle.

*Robbins, Mel. "How to stop screwing yourself over."
TEDx. 2011. Lecture.

Made in the USA
Lexington, KY
29 October 2019